D0291628

Ann,

Be a Mentor.

4/13/22

THE ART OF
MENTORING

Ravishankar Gundlapalli

TABLE OF CONTENTS

Foreword by **Sammy Lee**

思利及人 or Si Li Ji Ren, always considering others' interests, is the heart and soul of my family. Together with pragmatism, integrity, and constant entrepreneurship, Si Li Ji Ren runs through the veins of our business to remind us the importance of giving back to the community and sharing the fruits of our success. Growing up with these core values has not only shaped my leadership style but has also changed my outlook on life.

Mentoring is invaluable to me. My father Lee Man Tat was the pioneer of our family business' core values and was my first mentor. His lessons in life and business boosted my leadership skills and constantly reminded me to help others. As Winston Churchill famously said, "We make a living by what we get, but we make a life by what we give," our family is dedicated to paying our success forward and giving back to society.

Whether it's in the home, at the office, or in our community, our core values encourage us to engage different perspectives, to keep others' interest in mind, and to come up with solutions that benefit the collective. While my mentors have shared their teachings with me, I have become a mentor to others, and I hope that they can carry on the art of mentoring and sharing.

Mentoring is an integral channel for me to share my family's values like Si Li Ji Ren. That explains why I am so fascinated by Ravi's book *The Art of Mentoring*. It is about empowering others to achieve great results, to uphold important values, and to leverage their own strengths to succeed.

One of the goals for any leader is to reduce friction for employees to get things done. There are many reasons for the friction to occur. One main reason is what I call "insight gap" – knowing what is the right way to approach things in that particular context to solve a particular problem.

A thriving network of mentors can help employees to bridge this gap and to quickly learn the necessary skills to propel the organization to new heights. In my recent book *The Autopilot Leadership Model*, I talk at length about leveraging on each other's strengths. When you encourage such reciprocity of sharing and learning, it builds camaraderie and trust among your people and elevates the organization through synergy and collective wisdom.

Learning from another human being is powerful because it is both personal and contextual – an employee working on an RFP (Request For Proposal), or a student trying to get their first job, or an entrepreneur looking to win the first customer, or a senior executive looking to make a career change. In all these examples, learning from a mentor accelerates the learning process, which is a win-win for the individual as well as the organization as a whole.

I am delighted that Ravi has put together a guidebook to address both sides of the equation – how to help others as a mentor and how to receive help as a mentee. Being a good mentor and/or mentee is an important skill that is not taught in our traditional educational institutions today. I congratulate Ravi for providing a blueprint that people can refer to at any point in their career. There have been books on mentoring and on its power to transform organizations, but Ravi takes this one step deeper by discussing the best practices of engaging and building the most effective mentoring partnerships.

If you are someone who is aspirational and cares about others, then this book is for you. It will surely inspire you to help others and in the process become a more effective leader. Creating an effective mentoring network fosters a vigorous learning environment, promotes curiosity, and generates synergy to benefit all. Expand your definition of success beyond personal achievement because it is not all about the amount of wealth you build but the number of lives you have touched and helped that really matters.

Sammy Lee
Chairman & Managing Director
LKK Health Products Group Ltd
Author of *The Autopilot Leadership Model*

ADVANCE PRAISE

Creating new opportunities and building important relationships ranks high on most leaders' Project Lists. In "The Art of Mentoring," Dr. Gundlapalli provides us with not only the motivation we need to find our next mentor, but what to do when we sit down one on one. Sure you know that it takes a "Growth Mindset" to succeed and achieve your goals, but what do you DO to grow? Open this book, get started and watch your life change before your very eyes.

Jason W. Womack, MEd, MA

Cofounder: Get Momentum Leadership Academy

Author of *Get Momentum: How to start when you're stuck* and *Your Best Just Got Better*

"The Art of Mentoring is the perfect reminder that we don't have to figure it all out on our own."

Jodi Womack, MA

Cofounder: Get Momentum Leadership Academy

Author of *Get Momentum: How to start when you're stuck*

Ravi's passion to help bring Mentors and Mentees together will benefit the society at large significantly by creating better human beings, engineers and entrepreneurs. The secret of Mentorship is - most Mentors are willing to give their time for self motivated and passionate people. All that one has to do is to ask and show perseverance and sincerity, consistently.

Interestingly enough, most mentors will not even have an expectation that a mentee has to give back to the mentor. All that a mentor wants is a mentee to succeed in whatever they are doing.

So, if you are a person seeking mentorship, find the right mentor/s, ask and be sincere in your efforts. This book is an excellent guide for you to do everything right.

BV Jagadeesh

Managing Partner, KAAJ Ventures, Entrepreneur and Mentor

ACKNOWLEDGEMENTS

I consider myself to be incredibly lucky and blessed. I had not one, but two near-death experiences – first time was in my mother's womb six weeks before I eventually arrived, and the second time was in Feb 2009 when the plane I was on with 147 other passengers that nearly missed crashing into a helicopter carrying the President of India. I was old enough the second time to come away with the scary thought that if the plane did crash and all the 148 of us onboard died, who would the world talk about the most?

The second experience taught me two important lessons –

1) Life is precious

2) We are all here for a purpose to do something meaningful.

That purpose for me is to make mentoring an integral part of everyone's life and career.

My first mentors were my Mom and Dad who taught me the power of love, patience and hard work. My Dad built his career from scratch to become the top 100 insurance agents in India, and was a master at giving and helping others. When he passed away in 1999, hundreds of people came by to pay their respects and shared stories of how my Dad helped them in their lives and careers. So, it only seems natural to me now that I have written this book on *The Art of Mentoring*, as a guidebook for giving help and getting help from those we care for and those we respect.

I am deeply grateful to so many scholars, business leaders, teachers, professors, entrepreneurs, mentors, mentees, friends and family members who I have had the privilege of working with and having insightful conversations about mentoring. Each and everyone of them has taught me something new that I cherish dearly.

Can a cloud claim ownership of the water it holds? Can the same cloud tell us where each droplet of water came from? Neither can a mountain claim ownership of the water it receives nor the river that carries the water for long distances, enriching the earth and people along the way, before it merges into the ocean.

I feel the same way about the knowledge I am sharing with you in this book on *The Art of Mentoring*. It is a collection and summary of what I have heard, seen, learned, experienced and reflected upon.

However, there are a few oceans of knowledge that I want to specially acknowledge, and they include: Rajesh Setty, Prasad Kaipa, Sheila Forte-Trammell, Marla Gottschalk, BV Jagadeesh, Tony Tasca, Jason & Jodi Womack, Peter Lovgren, Sashi Chimala, Ranga Jayaraman, Santrupt Mishra, Mukul Agarwal, and Richie Norton. Every conversation with these individuals has enriched my knowledge of mentoring.

My deepest gratitude to Rajesh Setty who inspired me to write this book, and guided me at every step of the way. Rajesh never stops giving and is a living example of Si Li Ji Ren that Mr. Sammy Lee talks about in his Foreword to this book.

I would like to thank the Verbinden team of Satish Chapparike, Girish Kerodi, Vinay Kumar, Jerlin Johnson Biju, Saranya Bhaskaran who demonstrated so much patience and love for the work, and made this book possible.

Huge thanks to Tara May Flanagan who helped edit the final manuscript and gave excellent suggestions along the way. That she did all of this during a severe snow storm and without power in her house is incredible, and her heroic efforts demonstrate the power of teamwork when each and everyone on the team is connected to the cause and focused on the end goal.

I want to express my heartfelt gratitude to Jason Franzen from More Simple for his gift of creativity and genius with the cover design.

I would like to thank Sammy Lee, Chairman and Managing Director of LKK Health Products Group Ltd for writing the foreword for this book, and Jamie Lee for her help coordinating the same with great enthusiasm.

I am grateful to my guru Brahmasri Saamavedam Shanmukha Sarma, a true scholar and expert on Indian Vedas and countless other Indian literary texts. His blessings and immense wisdom continue to inspire and energize me.

The very essence of what I do everyday and the principles I live by are the result of my spiritual mentor Sri Sathya Sai Baba, and to him I offer my humble thanks and gratitude. His message of 'Love All – Serve All' is a recipe to bring joy to yourself and to everyone around you.

I want to thank my wife Vani who stood by me, with patience and love, and supported me immensely through ups and downs in this journey, as an entrepreneur and author. It is a true blessing to have a partner that believes in my vision and is willing to put up with everything that comes with it. Thanks to my daughter Nithya, an aspiring bioengineer and a mentor herself, for helping me choose the cover design and encouraging me to write this book as a valuable resource for her generation too. Vani and Nithya make my work worthwhile and add color to it every day.

There are so many other people that I want to thank but am unable to do so due to space constraints, but all of those that have helped me become who I am today have a place in my heart. One being our little dog Sparky, who was a constant companion during many late night sessions while I was working on this book.

There is still so much more to learn and share, and this book is only a humble beginning in my journey towards achieving my life's purpose. I am so delighted that you are a part of that journey now and hope you will read this book and refer to it time and again to give and get the most from your mentoring relationships. I sincerely welcome your feedback and suggestions. Be a mentor. Find a mentor. Change your world and the world around you.

Ravishankar Gundlapalli Ph.D.

San Jose, CA | Jan 2017

INTRODUCTION

Why should you read this book?

I wrote this book to share with you my 20+ years of experience in helping others, as well as receiving help from others. I didn't get to where I am alone; there were many individuals who held my hand and helped me along the way. Helping others is now a way for me to "pay it forward."

We can all identify at least one person who made a significant and positive impact on our lives. There could be—and most likely is— more than just one such individual in each of our lives. They changed our course and molded our thoughts. Those are our mentors, and they can be friends, relatives, co-workers, teachers, or known personalities. Our mentors are the more experienced, knowledgeable people in our lives who helped us stay on the right track by constantly guiding and nudging us along the way.

You have picked up this book because mentoring means something to you and is close to your heart. You enjoy helping others and sharing your knowledge and experience with people you care about. Or maybe you have heard stories of successful professionals and entrepreneurs, and how those people had the perfect mentors in their lives. You want to learn how they managed to win the attention and access to successful and caring individuals. It may also be that you believe in the power of mentoring and want to know how to bring that power to the organization or association you care about or are part of. Whatever the reasons might be, I am glad you are reading this book.

Mentoring is not a new idea. In fact, it is one of the oldest known methods for "positive and constructive influence" from one individual to another, and it is peppered throughout time in stories and in all cultures. The origin of the term *mentoring* dates back to the time of the ancient Greek storyteller, Homer. It is said that the modern use of the term however comes from the work of the 18th century French writer, Fenelon. Even in Hindu mythology, there are references to successful kings and scholars looking at certain individuals as their "mentors," separate from "teachers" or "gurus." In the ancient Indian epic, Mahabharata, the great warrior and leader, Arjuna, considered Lord Krishna as his mentor, and Sage Drona as his teacher. Drona taught Arjuna skills in archery and discipline, while Lord Krishna helped Arjuna understand the real world and make wise decisions at key points in his life, and was always there to help Arjuna. In Greek history, Alexander the Great considered Aristotle as his mentor.

A mentor is someone who "cares and shares." A mentee is someone who "trusts and acts." When you read these ancient stories, you begin to see how great leaders surrounded themselves both with those who taught them skills and others who shared wisdom.

Such an ancient and well-known human interaction as the mentor-mentee relationship is still relevant today. We read about successful entrepreneurs who attribute their success to receiving the right wisdom at the right time from people they trusted. Mark Zuckerberg and Steve Jobs are two prominent examples. Oprah Winfrey credits Maya Angelou, the celebrated author and poet, as her mentor. Musician Ray Charles was a mentor for the legendary musician Quincy Jones. Even Virgin Group co-founder Richard Branson wrote numerous articles about the influence mentors had on his own professional success.

your belief in yourself →

your mentor's belief in you.

IT WOULD BE A STRETCH FOR OTHERS TO BELIEVE IN YOU AT A LEVEL HIGHER THAN YOUR BELIEF IN YOURSELF. [YOUR MENTORS ARE AN EXCEPTION]

SOURCE: WWW·NAPKINSIGHT·COM/59

Companies have for decades adopted mentoring as a means to grow high potential employees into future leaders. Companies also leverage mentoring to advance women and minorities into leadership ranks. Leading entrepreneur networks like Y-Combinator, 500 Startups, Alchemist, Startups.co, Founder Institute, Boot Up World, and Unreasonable Institute, just to name a few, describe access to great mentors as one of their key value propositions for entrepreneurs.

Alumni networks across top-ranked global universities talk about engaging their successful alumni as mentors for recent graduates and current students. Movements like Million Women Mentors are on a mission to connect one million women working in STEM (Science, Technology, Engineering, Mathematics) careers with the up and coming generation of STEM professionals in universities and high schools across the United States of America.

My daughter Nithya was part of a mentoring program in high school where she acted as co-captain of the school's Speech & Debate team and was given the responsibility of passing on her skills and wisdom to the next batch of debaters from junior classes.

The value of mentoring has even made its way into pop culture: Who would Batman be without Alfred? Can you think of Luke without Yoda, or Po Kung Fu Panda without Master Shifu? Who would Harry Potter be without Dumbledore?

The references are endless. Suffice it to say that the power of mentoring is still going strong in today's organizations and institutions, and that this human practice of wisdom-transferring is at the core of what so many are doing to thrive and grow.

Unfortunately, there are still many misconceptions about what exactly mentoring is. I am dedicating an entire chapter to address these common myths about mentoring so that you are fully informed. I sincerely hope this book helps you start the conversation with those who challenge the power of mentoring, and allow you to become a champion of mentoring in your own professional and social networks.

Let us pause now and reflect on the following questions:

Do you enjoy helping others?

Do you have a skill or expertise that you believe others can benefit from?

Do you believe in sharing knowledge?

Do you enjoy being thanked for something you did for another person?

You are holding this book in your hands because your answers to these questions were a resounding YES.

Mentoring is a fundamental form of human development, where one person invests time, energy, and personal know-how in assisting the growth and capabilities of another person. A mentor is a person who identifies talent and ability within another person and helps bring those innate talents out, leading to self-discovery and mastery.

Mentoring comes in all shapes and sizes, and can start at an early age. If we reflect back on our own childhood and upbringing, mentoring actually begins at home with our mother and father as our first mentors. Legendary CEO of Cisco Systems, John Chambers, talks at length about the positive influence his mom and dad had on him. We can reflect on how our parents shaped us into who we are today. Those of us who are parents have the big responsibility of passing on our values, culture, and heritage to our children by being their first mentors.

What will be covered in this book?

This book will cover a few basic ideas and concepts related to mentoring. It will unwrap the secret that surrounds what mentoring is all about. In Chapter 2, you will get a deeper understanding of what mindset really is, and what kind of mindset mentors and mentees should have to build great mentoring relationships.

In Chapters 3 and 4, I will discuss how to be a good mentor and good mentee. These are fundamental skills for success that are not actively taught in our schools, colleges, or companies today. I want you to master these skills, and once you do, nothing can stand in your way of establishing your legacy and rapidly growing in your career.

Finding the right people to work with as a mentor or mentee can be a daunting task, and often intimidating. You can't possibly help everyone who comes your way; you just don't have the time and energy to do so. You also can't simply walk up to someone you respect and admire and ask, "Can you be my mentor?" Why should they? Why should they spend their valuable and irreplaceable time helping you? What's in it for them? In Chapter 5, I will present a 4-step process of how to find and work with the right mentors.

In Chapter 6, I will cover the core benefits of mentoring and how you can ensure you have a successful and rewarding mentoring relationship as a mentor and/or mentee. I will also share some insights on how to leverage mentoring relationships to create great stories that you can tell in your life.

What can you expect from this book?

By the time you reach the last page of this book, you will have gained the full meaning of a successful mentoring relationship, as well as proven best practices on how to be a good mentor or mentee that you can directly apply in your startup, education, or organization. Reading this book will help you learn how to give help, and how to get help. You will pick up several key skills and perspectives that you can successfully implement in your personal as well as professional lives.

Who should read this book?

I wrote this book with four kinds of people in mind. I have come across tens, sometimes hundreds, of people in each of these categories, and had the unique opportunity to be an observer, contributor, and beneficiary.

- *Aspiring Entrepreneurs* – You have big aspirations and want to change the world, but you cannot do it alone; you need the help of other people who can open doors for you. This book will show you how to leverage the art of mentoring in order to get help from the right people at the right time, and also how you can help other entrepreneurs.

- *Senior Executives* – Mentoring is a great way to demonstrate your leadership skills and leave a legacy. If you are 15-20 years into your career, you should start thinking about the story you will leave behind for others to tell. This book will help you learn how to build those stories, and ensure that you are remembered and recognized for many years to come.

- *Early to Mid-Career Employees* – You are either just getting started or settling down in your career, and mentoring is a skill you must leverage to connect with executives and the network of people around you. With this skill, you can ensure that you are learning and growing steadily and continuously in your career.

- *Students* – As you complete your education and look to launch your career, you should certainly explore on your own and create something new for yourself and the world. But you also want to be smart and make sure you avoid known mistakes by seeking guidance from others around you and from those who have been in your place. The art of mentoring is a skill that will help you get the best job, find happiness, and launch your career in the right way.

Welcome to the *Art of the Mentoring*. I have organized this book in such a way that each chapter is self-contained and can be read on its own, independent of the other chapters. My desire is that you will read this book not once, but again and again as you come back to it as a good reference for all your mentoring activities as a mentor and mentee.

1 ALL THINGS MENTORING

Before we get into the Art of Mentoring, I would like to first expand on all things mentoring. There are so many misconceptions and misinterpretations of what this word actually means and what exactly happens in a mentoring relationship.

Mentoring Unwrapped

Mentoring can be viewed in simple terms as a healthy, intellectual, and mutually rewarding conversation between two individuals. When I say two individuals, I am referring to one person having experience, skill, and competence in a particular domain, and another person who aspires to improve his or her game in that same domain. You can see that I am not at all referring to one individual being older or younger than the other. Age has no role to play here. What is at play is what I call 'Wisdom Asymmetry.'

One individual has a better grasp and knowledge than the other, and mentoring is a means of bridging that asymmetry in a positively reinforcing manner. Both individuals benefit in such a partnership founded on sharing and learning, and I will expand in future chapters on the benefits of mentoring to both mentors and mentees.

Mentoring in my own experience is a form of accelerated learning. There is a Japanese proverb that reads, "Better than a thousand days of diligent study is one day with a great mentor." There are times in our lives when we have to learn on our own, and other times when we must learn as fast as we can.

When you are in school, you are expected to learn the concepts by attending classes, reading the lessons on your own, and doing practice problems. At the end of the semester you are tested to demonstrate how much you have learned. If you have questions, you attend office hours with your teacher, or ask a fellow student to go over the concepts one more time so it improves your own understanding.

The situation is quite different when you work for a company or are building your startup as an entrepreneur. In a company, you are paid for your time, which means the company must do everything to make sure you learn the skills of the job quickly.

As an entrepreneur, time for you is money, and sometimes more than money. You want to pick up on key skills that you are lacking in as fast as you can so you can grow your company rapidly.

In each of these situations, getting help and guidance from the right individuals is vital to accelerating your learning and accomplishments.

A few words alone can work wonders when they are spoken with the right intent at the right time to the right audience.

SOURCE: WWW·NAPKINSIGHT·COM/97

When two individuals come together with the right intentions and trust, knowledge is sure to flow. That's exactly what mentoring is—a relationship of sharing and learning, happening simultaneously.

A day in the life of a

Startup & Corporate

Now that I have unwrapped what mentoring is all about, let me address the common myths surrounding mentoring. When a word is overused as much as the word 'mentoring', people tend to have their own interpretations and internalize it differently, many times incorrectly. I want to address these myths head-on before moving on to anything else. If there is one section you read in this book, let this be the one.

Common Myths around Mentoring

I have come across and spoken to thousands of students and professionals in my career. Over the last few years, mentoring is what I lived and breathed. In the process, I have identified four myths that are deeply entrenched in people's minds. Even people with decades of experience and phenomenal success under their belt still carry these misconceptions, and I am compelled to address them here.

Myth #1: Mentoring is only good for mentees

This is the most common misconception. People think that as a mentor, all you do is give to the other person, because you are such a generous, magnanimous person. But if you really dig deeper, it is you as the mentor who gains far more, because you are getting real validation for your knowledge. Your own understanding and expertise improves as a result of working with your mentees. You get to see how other people view the world, and the challenges they are facing. This is one instance where you get recognized for helping another individual overcome challenges and get ahead. As a mentor, you will also learn something new, because your mentees' situations or the challenges they face may force you to think differently. In a good mentoring relationship, you and your mentee can simultaneously learn from each other's strengths and experiences. A good mentoring relationship is never a one-way street.

I have posed this question to hundreds of highly successful professionals: "Can you imagine leaving this planet with all the wisdom and experience in your head?" 100% of the time, I get a nice chuckle as a response and a big NO! Being a mentor is a great way to avoid keeping all of your knowledge with yourself. The beauty of sharing knowledge is that your knowledge not only remains within you, but also grows, while transferring huge benefits to other people. This is unlike sharing time or money, which you lose once you give them away.

In a recent conversation with Sheila Forte-Trammell, former global chief of mentoring at IBM and co-author of *Intelligent Mentoring: How IBM Creates Value Through People, Knowledge and Relationships,*" Sheila said, "Mentoring is a way to see your profession thrive long after you are gone." What an amazing and deep statement. Who would want to be the last teacher, the last engineer, the last entrepreneur, the last artist, the last doctor, the last musician, or the last soccer player, etc., on the planet? No one! That is why mentoring is good for mentors, too.

Myth #2: Mentoring takes a lot of time (for mentors)

Another big misconception I often hear from mentors is that mentoring takes too much time. And yes, I agree, any activity that is worth doing takes time. But in this busy world we live in, we have a way of finding time for those activities we enjoy, or for tasks that we *have* to do. People who claim they do not have time for mentoring are actually saying that they do not see value in mentoring.

If you choose the right mentoring matches from the start, the time you spend building those relationships will bring you nothing but immense value. A powerful mentoring conversation can be as short as five-to-ten minutes over the phone or video chat. Or it can happen over a 20-minute meeting with a clear agenda and focused conversation. The value lies in the quality of time spent, not the quantity. The value of mentoring should be measured by the incremental benefits generated for the mentee and the mentor, and not by the time spent by either of them. When you look at mentoring in this way, time will not become a factor or an excuse to say no to mentoring. I will share some examples of this in future chapters.

In my case, I spend an average of 30 minutes every other week with three or four of my mentees at any one time. I consider my time and conversations with mentees as my time away from my own work, and an opportunity to help others grow. I learn a lot from my mentees. My mentees make me feel valued for the knowledge I have, and what I am able to do for them. I feel a sense of *accomplishment* when I achieve success in my own pursuits. Working with my mentees and seeing them move ahead in their careers or startups gives me a sense of *significance*, which is priceless and worth my time. Thanks to mentoring, I have real stories to tell in my talks and interviews.

If you look at mentoring as a strategic way to grow in your career, it can be a lot of fun, and well worth your time, too. If you approach mentoring in this way, and when you master the concepts in this book, I hope you will never claim that you do not have enough time for mentoring. You will actually make time to get help and to help others.

Myth #3: Mentoring is not a mainstream topic

Most media coverage surrounding mentoring in the 1990's and 2000's was related to social situations, e.g., mentoring for minorities, helping disadvantaged populations, and mentoring women to increase diversity in the workforce. But when I interviewed successful entrepreneurs and executives about the one thing that helped them become who they are today, I found there was far more to the story. Universally, they all talked about other key individuals—fellow entrepreneurs, former CEOs or bosses, professors—who had an impact on them by helping to navigate their careers and teaching them to make key decisions at critical points during their careers. Take for example, Indra Nooyi, Chairman and CEO of Pepsico. In a 2008 interview*, she said "If I hadn't had mentors, I wouldn't be here today. I am a product of great mentoring and great coaching." Nooyi relates a personal story of how Pepsico's then president, Steve Reinemund, played a key role in steering her career trajectory towards eventually gaining the broad experience she needed to be named as the Chairman and CEO.

I discussed several other examples in the Introduction of this book. Even Aristotle, Plato, Beethoven, Einstein—all considered great men and experts in their lines of work—sought guidance and wisdom from mentors. We simply cannot solve every problem and obstacle that comes our way; sometimes we require the intelligence and perspective of others to find our way. Mentoring has always been—and should remain—a mainstream topic.

*YouTube Video: *Indra Nooyi States Importance of Listening To Your Mentors*

Myth #4: Mentoring cannot be done online

Before the Internet, everything we did was restricted to the physical world. Talking to friends, shopping, meeting someone, sharing photos, applying for jobs or attending an interview—everything required us to be physically present. With technology, all that has changed. Even dating went online with the phenomenal success of sites like Match.com, eHarmony, Tinder. We live in a highly connected world where distance no longer matters.

In exactly the same way, mentoring can be conducted online and virtually; all it takes is for two individuals from any part of the world to trust each other's knowledge, aspirations, and values, and have the desire to connect and have conversations with the purpose of learning from each other. I have had mentees as far away as India who I have worked with actively. Distance is not a factor when it comes to understanding what another person needs, and then being able to provide resources, perspective, and new opportunities for them.

Mentoring is certainly more powerful when conducted in person, but it should not be restricted to face-to-face interactions, especially in today's highly connected world. What if the person who can best help you lives in a different zip code, or city, or even country? What if you do not live in big cities or economic hubs like Silicon Valley or London or Dubai or Tokyo, and live in a distant small town or village?

In 2012, U.S. Secretary of State Hillary Rodham Clinton invited me to deliver a plenary talk, and I chose to speak on 'Mentoring Beyond Borders,' where professionals defy geographical limits to mentor youth and students in all parts of the world. Mentors are able to create significant impact by transferring wisdom across borders, without actually having to travel there physically. The idea was acknowledged widely, and today it is actually happening at one of my companies, MentorCloud, where mentors and mentees are connecting across geographical locations.

In summary, mentoring is

- Beneficial to mentors
- A valuable and rewarding use of your time, if done properly
- A strategic approach to accelerating your learning and career
- Equally valuable and impactful in-person or online

1.3. Is Mentoring for Everyone?

History shows that most successful people have had one or more mentors who have had a phenomenal impact on their career.

As human beings, we all have something to share and something to learn, so we can all benefit from mentorship. There is always more that you don't know in this world than you do know. Mentoring enables you to share what you know and what you are passionate about, as well as learn what you need to know in order to get ahead in your career. Mentoring is a form of learning and sharing that is not restricted to any certain time in your career.

You could be in high school, college, early career, starting a business, late career, or retired. No matter which phase in life you find yourself in, you can benefit from powerful mentoring relationships.

2   MENTORING MINDSET

Let me now talk about mindset. The right mindset is so important for success in mentoring, whether you are a mentor or a mentee. Having the wrong mindset will stunt a new mentoring relationship from the get-go, preventing both mentor and mentee from accomplishing the goals they set for themselves. On the other hand, having the right mindset will kick start the mentorship into a powerful relationship that fosters learning and growth for both individuals.

Several years ago, I watched an inspiring INK talk titled, 'Singing in the life boat', by Aisha Choudhary. Aisha was just 15 years old when she delivered the talk, and battling a life-threatening medical condition called Pulmonary Fibrosis. She unfortunately passed away in January 2015, but some of her statements and approach to life have left an indelible impression on me. In her talk, Aisha said, *"You live every moment twice, once in your mind and once when you actually live it.*" How true her words are! Aisha's statement relates perfectly to the mindset required for a successful mentoring relationship.

So what constitutes the "right" mindset? According to professor Carol Dweck, author of *Mindset: The New Psychology of Success,* there are two primary types of mindset: A Fixed Mindset (FM) and a Growth Mindset (GM).

After drawing a lot of inspiration from her writings, I reached out to Carol and had the privilege of meeting her in person and having multiple conversations about my work in the area of mentoring. I told Carol that her book helped me make an important connection between mindset and mentoring. I was even able to convince her to be a strategic advisor during the early years of my company, MentorCloud.

Types of Mindset

To understand the connection between mindset and mentoring, it is important for you to know a bit more about the two types of mindsets that Carol talks about.

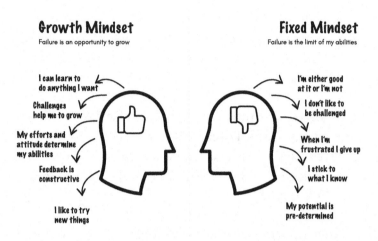

Fixed Mindset

People with a fixed mindset believe that their innate intelligence and skills *should* give them the rewards they deserve. People with a fixed mindset believe that they have been gifted with certain skills, knowledge, and intellectual capacity, and they are *supposed* to be successful. If they don't become successful, they become angry and blame everyone and everything around them. They feel entitled to success. They think that the world is being unfair to them if they do not achieve what they are seeking. They think that the world is out to get them, and they get frustrated. They tend to give up very easily.

Carol gives many examples of C-level executives losing their temper during meetings when their ideas are not implemented, and of tennis players breaking their rackets when their shots are called out by the referee. She especially talks a lot about children and how parents should not over-praise their children for being smart in something, because this tends to develop in children a fixed mindset. Carol instead encourages parents to praise their children's efforts. Students who think they are successful because of their smartness, Carol says, are less likely to accept failure, and do not learn from mistakes and criticism. If, on the other hand, parents attribute their children's success to hard work and effort, they are more likely to try harder, and eventually achieve a higher degree of success.

Growth Mindset

People with a growth mindset take a different approach. They might say: "Yes I have been granted certain skills and innate intellectual capacity, but if I don't work hard and put in the necessary effort, I may not be successful." People with a growth mindset focus on their own effort, over and above the skills they have been gifted with. For example, a student with a growth mindset will see a lower-than-expected grade as an opportunity to work harder and do better. Such students neither blame their teachers for giving them a lower grade, nor develop a false belief that they are not good enough in a particular subject.

I can give another example where one employee is passed over by another employee for a promotion. Employees with a fixed mindset are likely to think they have been wronged, whereas someone with a growth mindset will reflect and find ways to improve in order to be considered for a promotion in the future.

Effort is a far better guarantor of success than innate talent alone. Even the greatest prodigies in music or sports spend thousands of hours practicing their craft. In his best-selling book, *Outliers*, Malcolm Gladwell talks at length about the 10,000-hour rule to gain total mastery in a particular field.

Mindset of a good Mentor and Mentee

A mentoring partnership will only be successful if both the mentor and mentee have a growth mindset. The mentor should believe that the mentee can learn and grow. The mentee should also believe that they can learn and grow with the advice and guidance of their mentor.

Good mentors are those with more business experience in a particular domain, and they should have the faith that their mentees can learn and build their competencies over time. Without a growth mindset, mentors can become frustrated when they do not see results quickly enough.

On the other hand, good mentees should have the attitude of a student, with a willingness to learn and grow. If mentees instead approach the relationship with a fixed mindset, they are likely to miss important feedback and insights from their mentors. Such mentees tend to move from one mentor to the next, until they find someone who agrees with them. Having a mentor that always agrees with you may not always lead to positive results.

Whether you are a mentor or mentee, maintaining a growth mindset is a foundational skill. It will create the right conditions for magic to happen, and you will find your mentoring relationships to be extremely rewarding and satisfying.

3   WHAT GOOD MENTORS DO

"A truly great mentor is hard to find, difficult to part with, and impossible to forget."

– Anonymous

Besides having a growth mindset, what exactly are the characteristics of good mentors? It is important to familiarize yourself with various traits of good mentors so that you, too, can be conscious of them during your own mentoring interactions. Using some or all of these traits will help you become a good—and eventually a great—mentor.

Good mentors change lives, period. From all my mentoring interactions and conversations with good mentors, I identified 14 core traits by which good mentors change the lives of their mentees.

1. Open new doors and expand possibilities

2. Identify and amplify strengths

3. Increase confidence level

4. Ask great questions and help with prioritization

5. Prevent emotional decision making

6. Move the needle

7. Teach how to tell the story better

8. Be committed to the relationship

9. Provide a comfortable environment

10. Share and care

11. Have compassion

12. Listen without being judgmental

13. Be inspiring

14. Be a sounding board

#1 – Good mentors open new doors and expand possibilities

Good mentors tap into their own professional networks and connect their mentees with key individuals, creating lasting and valuable connections. Each of you may have 500 or 1000 connections on LinkedIn, and perhaps many more in your own private circles. But you do not reach out to many of them on a regular basis, because you do not have a need at that particular point in your career.

Now, bring in the needs of your mentees and, suddenly, you may find some of those connections to be very valuable to your mentee. I can share an example from my own experience: In late 2008, I started mentoring a visually challenged student, Srikanth Bolla, who hails from a small village in India, who at that time was seeking help to get into his dream college, MIT (Massachusetts Institute of Technology in Cambridge USA). After being turned away by so many people, he wanted to prove himself. I met him serendipitously at a conference in Hyderabad, India, and I decided to mentor him after being impressed by his talents, previous accomplishments, and strong desire to succeed.

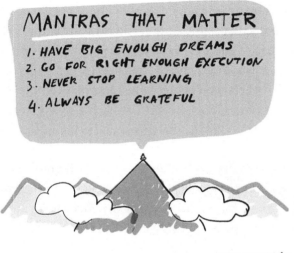

SOURCE: WWW.NAPKINSIGHTS.COM/24

Over the next few years working with Srikanth, I was able to connect him with a handful of people in my network who were able to help him reach his goals. For example, one of my longtime friends, Satish Vedala, had started a foundation in his mother's name to support people with disabilities. Srikanth's need for a financial grant brought to mind Satish's foundation, and I was able to connect the two. That connection led to a valuable relationship in which Satish's foundation provided the funding for Srikanth's travels to the United States to study at MIT.

I have personally benefited from such connections opened by my mentors. Rajesh Setty is a very successful entrepreneur, prolific author, and my mentor for over five years. He connected me to several people in his network, some of whom eventually invested in my projects, and several others who became great partners. Before Rajesh opened those doors, he did not have a specific need for those contacts, but he saw their value to me as his mentee.

Rajesh also connected me to the Isha Foundation, led by Sadhguru Jaggie Vasudev, which opened many new doors for me to expand my mentoring work to entrepreneurs and professionals in India.

These examples demonstrate the value of opening doors for your mentees by connecting them with key people in your network. Take a moment to look at each of your current mentoring relationships and complete the blanks below:

Mentee name	Mentee's immediate need	Names of 5 people who can help
1		
2		
3		
4		
5		

#2 – Good mentors identify and amplify mentees' strengths

No one is perfect and everyone has strengths and weaknesses. Good mentors help mentees recognize their innate strengths. Once a mentee is aware of his or her strengths, it becomes a lot easier to leverage those strengths in particular situations, and to achieve mastery over time.

In psychology, they talk about four stages of competence for individuals progressing from incompetence to competence in a particular skill or activity.

Stage 1: Unconscious Incompetence – You don't know what you don't know. You are not even aware that a certain skill that is fundamentally needed for you to succeed is something you don't even have. This is like a blind spot that you yourself don't see or recognize.

Stage 2: Conscious Incompetence – You know what you don't know. You are now fully aware that you lack skill and competence in a particular area, and that you need to do something about it. By knowing what you don't know, you will be more careful about the situations you put yourself in, to make sure you don't embarrass yourself. Now that you know, you are likely to be on the lookout for resources to learn.

Stage 3: Conscious Competence – You know what you know. You are fully aware of specific skills needed, and you have already taken the necessary training, coaching, and mentoring to improve your performance in those skills. You are operating *in the zone* after being trained and mentored, but you are doing so 'consciously.' In this stage, you can confidently put yourself in situations that demand those skills, and deliver great performance.

Stage 4: Unconscious Competence – You don't know what you know. You are operating in the zone of your innate strengths, and you are not even aware of being *in the zone*. You are delivering a natural performance and doing so 'unconsciously.' You have perhaps been acknowledged widely for your performance, but in your mind you believe that everyone should be good at this. You don't see what is so special about you, or why people are getting so excited about what you are doing.

Good mentors make it their priority to familiarize themselves with these stages, and to use them when working with their mentees.

First, good mentors look for Stage 4 skills in their mentees, i.e., innate strengths, and call them out. They encourage their mentees to proactively place themselves in situations where their strengths will be acknowledged and rewarded.

In my own experience, Rajesh helped me realize my natural presentation skills, especially when I am on stage. He noticed that without much preparation, I am able to connect with the audience and give insightful answers to questions. Soon after he made me realize this, I magically found myself invited to be on panels and speak at conferences in the USA, Europe, and India, and I did very well. This very book is a result of Rajesh calling out my ability to articulate my ideas in words, and encouraging me to write a book.

Second, good mentors also help mentees recognize specific skills that fall under Stage 1, i.e., skills they don't have and are not even aware of it. The mentees are making mistakes that are visible to their mentors and others, but not to themselves. Identifying a Stage 1 skill is excellent, especially if mentees accept the feedback with a growth mindset, as discussed in Chapter 2.

OOPS!

EVERYONE MAKES MISTAKES. THOSE WHO WANT TO LEARN & GROW ADMIT THEIR MISTAKES READILY

SOURCE : WWW · NAPKINSIGHTS.COM /231

It is only once mentees are made aware of certain shortcomings, such as the way they give presentations, or their posture during a presentation, or improper understanding of competition, or speaking too fast, etc., that they can begin to improve on those specific skills (move to Stage 2). Good mentors then provide access to learning resources and work with their mentees to improve their skills so they can move into Stage 3 competence. This is where mentees are now aware of the mistakes they are likely to commit, and consciously use the newly gained skills to avoid those mistakes. The mentees become like actors on stage, fully prepared for their act.

#3 – Good mentors increase the confidence level of mentees

Good mentors encourage their mentees to feel comfortable and strong as they are. They do not say to their mentees, "You can't do this, you can't do that." Instead, they focus on what mentees CAN do. No one can do everything—that's a fact of life. But great mentors identify certain aspects and say, "Hey, what if we did this? Can you do this? Have you tried doing this?" They work on building self-esteem in their mentees. Anyone who is an entrepreneur, or a student, or in the early stages of their career, will experience ups and downs. But great mentors help their mentees see through the clutter, gain confidence in themselves, and focus on their efforts.

One way good mentors do this is by sharing stories from their own careers, or anecdotes of others who might have gone through a similar situation as the mentee. Knowing that they are not alone in their struggles, and that others who faced the same challenges came out successful, will be reassuring and inspiring to their mentees.

When I work with a student or an entrepreneur, I always focus on what they are capable of doing and where their true potential is. I make it a point to highlight any Stage 4 skills, and I let my mentees know how special it is to possess such skills. People like to be acknowledged for the skills they have, rather than be put down for the skills they don't have. It's the age-old idea of looking at a glass of water and deciding whether it is half full or half empty.

Good mentors always see the glass as half full. Mr. Narendra Modi, Hon Prime Minister of India, offers an even more interesting take on this idea: the glass is half full with water and half full with air. Good mentors remember that their mentees have unique skills of their own, and that it is their job to take the time to identify those skills and help their mentees become aware of them.

#4 – Good mentors ask great questions and help their mentees prioritize

Good mentors make 1+1 seem like 11. When mentees come up with new ideas about their career or business or education, good mentors listen to them and let them expand on those ideas. By asking the right probing questions in a polite way, good mentors encourage mentees to talk through their ideas. They give their mentees the time necessary to explain their ideas in full without interrupting them.

The flow of thought is very important, and sometimes all it takes to keep the flow going is a simple 'tell me more.' Once mentees have finished sharing their ideas and plans, then good mentors suggest additions or changes in direction by offering in their own perspective.

In this case, asking the right questions is key to encouraging mentees to express themselves. Here are some examples of questions good mentors ask:

- Have you thought about ….
- Why do you think....
- What if you approached....
- Are there other ways you can accomplish the same....

- What would you recommend if you were in my shoes....

- Which path do you feel most comfortable with.....

- Can you think of ways in which your assumptions can be wrong....

- What if you partnered with .....

It's impossible to overstate the immense value good mentors add by asking the right questions at the right time, with the intent of bringing clarity to their mentees' thinking. Mentors may not have all the answers, but the process helps mentees to find the right answers by themselves and use those answers to effectively prioritize what to do next.

The process of prioritization also involves helping mentees connect their actions with their targeted goals and milestones. At any given time, you will have many activities to do in order to move ahead with your startup or career. The challenge is deciding which of those activities will give you the results you are looking for. Good mentors teach mentees how to connect activities to results, helping their mentees find a clear process for prioritization.

#5 – Good mentors prevent mentees from making emotional decisions

Good mentors teach a decision process that is more structured and less emotional. Most people can't help but become emotionally attached to their ideas or plans; it's just part of being human. So when a mentee comes to their mentor in a heightened mental state, good mentors ask the right questions.

The intent of good mentors is to build two key skills in their mentees: 'decision-making,' and 'decision-abiding.'

First, mentees are encouraged to explain how they arrived at their strategy or action plan. They are asked to list five reasons why they should go with a particular plan or decision, followed by five reasons why they shouldn't. This process forces the mentee to learn to think deeply instead of moving ahead purely on emotion. Over time, mentees will build the key skill of 'decision-making.'

But making a decision is not enough by itself. Once a decision is made, the mentees also need to be taught how to abide and stand by their decision. Feeling a sense of remorse or guilt or anger when a decision goes wrong is not helpful. If the decision-making process is in order, then mentees can always go back to the reasons why they made a particular decision in the first place, strengthening their decision-abiding skill.

#6 – Good mentors move the needle for mentees

Rajesh taught me that real mentoring is about moving the needle; i.e., helping mentees accomplish something. Mentoring cannot be an exercise in intellectual entertainment where you as the mentor ask tough questions and leave mentees to find answers on their own. Asking questions is perfectly fine and highly recommended, but good mentors also bear the responsibility of making sure that their mentees have a way to find answers.

Leaving their mentees puzzled, confused, and dazzled with their intelligence is not what good mentors do. For good mentors, mentoring is not an opportunity to display their intelligence. Real mentoring is a mutual conversation where the intelligence and experience of mentors coupled with the aspirations of mentees is leading the mentees to move closer to a particular goal or milestone.

At the end of every conversation or email exchange with my mentees, I make sure they get connected to a new person or resource, or that they've come up with a new deliverable to work on.

#7 – Good mentors help mentees tell their stories better

Not all of us are born storytellers, and today's world is all about storytelling. How you present yourself and your career goals is extremely important, and even more important than the actual details themselves. A story has the power to touch the heart of the listener or the viewer. The situation could be a job interview, or pitching to an investor, or writing an essay for college. In each of these situations, it is about how you tell your story.

While you are honing your storytelling skills to influence others, there are people out there who are using their storytelling skills to influence their own advantage

SOURCE : WWW.NAPKINSIGHTS.COM /35

One of my good friends, Joseph Prabhakar, once told me about a story formula that Hollywood follows to a T. He called it the 3S model:

Situation – Show what the world is like today

Struggle – Bring in a 3rd party and describe the problems created as a result

Solution – Now present the solution to the problems created and demonstrate how the situation has improved

In a similar fashion, mentors teach their mentees how to tell their story in a way that is compelling and captivating to listeners. In the process, mentors help mentees build the skill of storytelling, which they can use repeatedly throughout the course of their career.

#8 – Good mentors are committed to their mentees' success

Being a mentor for someone is very gratifying. If being committed to one's own goals and aspirations is ordinary, showing commitment to another individual's goals and aspirations is truly extraordinary.

Good mentors demonstrate this commitment by investing the time necessary to make their mentees successful. It is not the quantity of time spent with mentees that counts, but the quality of time. Good mentors are conscious of this fact, and constantly look for ways to increase the capacity of their mentees. Such a commitment triggers the desire to take action, which moves the needle for the mentees.

STANDARDS

There is no fine for raising your own standards.

Go Ahead - you will be just fine!

SOURCE: WWW.NAPKINSIGHTS.COM/258

In short, good mentors don't enter into a partnership unless they are ready to make that commitment. There are plenty of ways good mentors demonstrate such commitment: tap into their network and see who the mentees should be talking to; suggest a book that the mentees should read; recommend a video the mentees should watch; or suggest an event the mentees should attend. None of these suggestions by mentors take more than a few minutes, but all of them have the potential to significantly change the game for the mentees.

To illustrate, let me share a recent experience. BV Jagadeesh is a very successful serial entrepreneur, and someone I consider as a role model and mentor. He always makes time for me and asks great questions, which have helped me become a better entrepreneur. In late 2016, over a 10-minute meeting, BV suggested that I meet with Ajay from BootUP, a premier startup community in Silicon Valley. That one door that BV opened changed the game for me and my company, MentorCloud, and put us on a rapid growth path.

BV opened that door because of his deep inner commitment to making sure I am successful in my entrepreneurial journey. I used to hear from other entrepreneurs in the Valley that BV talked about me and my company in some of his conversations and presentations, which is another demonstration of how a good mentor like BV shows his commitment to his mentee's success.

#9 – Good mentors make mentees comfortable with being vulnerable

Success for mentees comes only when they are open and vulnerable with their mentors, and comfortable with discussing challenges. How can any mentor help if they are not aware of their mentees' challenges?

Good mentors offer a safe environment that makes mentees feel comfortable with sharing challenges. Such mentors consciously avoid being intimidating, or demanding, or making their mentees feel low.

Good mentors take note when mentees say that everything is fine and that there are no challenges. This is a sign that mentees are not yet feeling comfortable enough to open up. Even Bill Gates, who can be counted among the greatest business leaders of all time, shared that he needed someone like Warren Buffet to turn to for guidance in times of crisis and vulnerability.

#10 – Good mentors share and care for mentees

Good mentors share and care. Good mentees trust and act. Good mentors share what they know or who they know with sincere care for their mentees' success. Because they care, good mentors make sure that whatever they are sharing is meaningful, timely, and useful for the mentees.

I will share an example of what my mentor, Dr. Tony Tasca, does. Tony is a well-respected organizational development and human resources executive, with over 50 years of experience under his belt. When Tony comes across an interesting article or book, he forwards it to me, and sometimes even prints a hard copy just to make sure I don't miss reading it.

In one of my recent meetings with Tony, he gave me the names and emails of five people from his network that I should reach out to. This, in my opinion, is a demonstration of Tony's care for me through sharing his knowledge and connections.

#11 – Good mentors show compassion towards their mentees

Compassion is an important quality of good mentors. Previously, I talked about sharing with caring, and also providing a comfortable environment for mentees, but none of this will work in the absence of compassion.

Good mentors are grateful to those who have helped them along the way. This gratitude allows mentors to see themselves in their mentees, and to be more understanding and compassionate.

Being compassionate means that good mentors are able to relate to their mentees' situation and challenges, and are able to put themselves in their mentees' shoes. Good mentors take time to understand the circumstances in which their mentees are operating, and by doing so, they are in a better position to provide the right kind of guidance, and eventually move the needle for their mentees.

You cannot kick the ladder after you finish climbing it. Good mentors know this well, and it is where their compassion takes root.

#12 – Good mentors listen to their mentees without being judgmental

Good mentors are good listeners. They have the capability to hear what their mentee is saying and also not saying—a little like reading between the lines.

The human mind has a bad habit of not listening when it's judging the speaker or waiting for a pause so it can interject. Because the mind is busy processing a response, it is no longer listening to what is being said, and, more importantly, *how* it is being said.

By allowing mentees to speak without interruption, mentors encourage mentees to devise answers to their own questions, or identify potential holes in their arguments and positioning. Good mentors combine good listening skills with compassion, and become very valuable partners in their mentees' success.

#13 – Good mentors inspire their mentees

The key role of a mentor is to inspire, not to influence. The word 'inspire' is a powerful word, and I learned its true meaning from Dr. Lance Secretan, one of the most insightful leadership gurus of the 21st century. Lance is the author of 15 amazing books, including, *Inspire, The Spark, the Flame, and the Torch, ONE, The Way of the Tiger,* and many more.

During the early days of MentorCloud, I had the unique privilege of spending a day with Lance and his wife, Tricia, in their lovely home in Colorado. It was a life-changing experience for me, and if I am still working on my life's mission of connecting 100 million mentors and mentees by 2020, it is because of that inspiring day with Mr. and Mrs. Secretan.

Lance explained to me how people often confuse the meaning of the words motivate and inspire, and I was one of them. Lance taught me that the word motivate comes from the Latin root word 'mot', which means 'move'. The word inspire, on the other hand, comes from the Latin word 'inspirare', which means 'breathe into.' I listened to him that day like a child learning the alphabet for the first time.

When you motivate someone, you are making them do something because of a follow-up incentive or reward. Motivation, then, requires some external force, energy, or incentive to make a person take action.

When you inspire a person, you are making them *want* to do something on their own. You are able to do this because you are breathing positive energy into the other individual, who then takes action on their own. If you do this correctly, no force or energy or incentive is required from you, since the other person is moving forward with their own energy.

Inspiration should not be an act, but a habit. I have been told by many people that they are inspired by what I say and do. I have reflected on what exactly makes me an inspiration to others and identified these six behaviors:

1. Be authentic and genuine.
2. Share my stories with passion, emotion, and honesty.
3. Talk about others who inspired me and made me who I am today.
4. Boldly talk about my life's mission and vision.

5. Discuss my life's successes and failures, and show my vulnerability.

6. Show genuine care and offer hope to the other person.

Good mentors exhibit these behaviors naturally, which inspires their mentees. Knowing this, you can consciously build these behaviors in your own mentoring interactions.

One of my favorite poets is Sirivennela Seetarama Sastry, who hails from Southern India. I had a unique opportunity to meet with Sastry one-on-one. A statement of his touched me so deeply that it has become one of the foundations of my aspirations and how I live my life. Translated from Telugu to English, he said, "True success in life should be measured not by how many forts you build, but in how many hearts you reside."

Good mentors find a place in their mentees' hearts, and continuously breathe new energy from within.

#14 – Good mentors validate ideas and act as a sounding board

Good mentors become the first point of validation for mentees to discuss new ideas. By having an intellectual and engaging conversation, and with all of the traits described above, good mentors help mentees develop more clarity on their ideas or situation.

By reflecting on their professional and personal experiences, good mentors provide real feedback to their mentees' ideas, rather than simply rejecting a particular idea.

Everyone sees the world with their own eyes. What one person sees and infers from the image on their retina is not exactly the same as another person. Good mentors recognize this.

When I was launching MentorCloud, I came across many people who said the idea would not work. I felt disappointed, initially, until I listened to Chris Gardner at a conference in Los Angeles, California (USA) and learned something fundamental.

Chris Gardner is an innovator, successful entrepreneur, stockbroker, and philanthropist whose early life as a homeless person was published as an autobiography titled, *In Pursuit of Happiness*. His life story was also depicted in the movie with the same name. At the conference, Chris introduced the power of mentoring and talked about being bold and never taking No for an answer. He reasoned that the person giving you a No may not be seeing what you are seeing, and may not know how to make your idea work as much as you can.

When someone tells you that your idea will not work, they are actually saying that they don't know how to make the idea work. Good mentors never reject ideas, and instead help mentees discover the pros and cons of their ideas on their own, and encourage them to try. One of Nelson Mandela's famous quotes is, "*It always seems impossible until it's done.*"

Summary – What Good Mentors Do

I have described 14 key behaviors of good mentors. I hope you will build these behaviors so that you, too, can become a good—and eventually great—mentor. Remember that improving your mentoring skills is a continuous process.

Offering yourself as a mentor to someone is the best thing you can do to demonstrate your leadership, to be recognized for your expertise, and to establish your legacy. I'll go even further and say that being a mentor for someone is your duty to help your family, profession, community, and country thrive. Someone did it for you, whether you realize it or not.

Now that you have learned about all 14 traits of good mentors, I would like you to remember these in the form of a pledge, and refer back to this list every once in a while, in your own mentoring interactions. Place a checkmark next to the statement every time you review it, as my goal for you is to become a Stage 4 competent mentor.

Mentor Pledge

As a good mentor –

I will – Open new doors and expand possibilities for my mentees

I will – Identify and amplify the strengths of my mentees

I will – Increase the confidence level of my mentees

I will – Ask great questions and help my mentees prioritize

I will – Prevent my mentees from making emotional decisions

I will – Help my mentees to move the needle

I will – Teach my mentees how to tell their story better

I will – Be committed to the success of my mentees

I will – Make my mentees comfortable with being vulnerable

I will – Share and care for my mentees

I will – Show compassion towards my mentees

I will – Listen to my mentees without being judgmental

I will – Inspire my mentees

I will – Be a sounding board for my mentees

4 WHAT GOOD MENTEES DO

Being a mentee essentially means that you have the desire to become better at what you do, and are ready to do whatever necessary to take your game to the next level. You are willing to learn from those you trust, and put that learning into practice.

Learning as a mentee is not exactly the same as learning as a student. As a student, you are taught new concepts in particular subjects, and then tested on those concepts to make sure you have grasped the basic ideas behind the concepts. On the other hand, as a mentee, you are taught how to put the concepts you have learned into practice, or into a particular context.

It takes a different set of skills to be a great mentee, and I will describe them here. These six habits empower good mentees to draw the most benefits when working with their mentors:

1.   Trust and take action

2.   Provide regular updates

3.   Be grateful

4.   Proactively offer help

5.   Have a growth mindset

6.   Maintain confidentiality of conversations

#1 – Good mentees trust their mentors and take action

As a mentee, you can't learn anything meaningful if you don't have trust in your mentors. In his best-selling book, *The Speed of Trust: The One Thing That Changes Everything*, author Stephen M.R. Covey describes trust as a 'critical, highly relevant, performance multiplier.'

Good mentees multiply their own performance by having a deep appreciation for their mentors' expertise and values, and by trusting in their mentors. They do enough research on their mentors prior to entering into a formal mentoring partnership, ensuring they are prepared and ready to take advice.

When there is complete trust between a mentee and mentor, the output of the partnership will be far greater than if there is a lack of trust. Trust builds bridges and allows wisdom to flow freely between you and your mentor.

While it is essential to a successful mentoring partnership, trust is not enough by itself. Good mentees also take action on the advice and guidance provided by their mentors. They realize that nothing happens if they don't act on that advice, or follow up on any doors that their mentors have opened for them.

Good mentees know that their mentors will lose interest in the partnership if they don't take action and provide timely updates, which is the 2nd behavior I am going to talk about next.

#2 – Good mentees provide regular updates to their mentors

Being accountable to the mentoring partnership is important for both the mentor and the mentee. Remember that both the mentor and mentee are investing time in the partnership.

Time is a challenge for all of us. I never seem to find enough time to do everything I want to do. I can replace money, but I cannot replace time. Time can never be regained. If someone is willing to share some of their precious time with me, the least I should do is provide them with regular updates on my progress. This is what good mentees do, constantly.

Good mentees keep their mentors in the loop on an ongoing basis, and share their results. If something is not working, they let their mentors know right away. Your responsiveness and diligence will send a message to your mentors that you respect their time. Hearing positive results from you will also make your mentors happy about the time they are giving you.

Good mentees do not just listen and go away, or go silent on their mentors for weeks at a time. This is sure to disappoint the mentors. Good mentees are also up front with their mentors, and let them know when the relationship is not working out.

Sending updates is also a subtle way for good mentees to keep their mentoring relationships active. Mentors can get busy with their own careers and companies, and may even have other mentees that they are working with. By staying engaged and accountable, good mentees succeed in getting more of their mentors' attention. Another side benefit of providing regular updates is that you remain on the mind of your mentors, so they can talk about you to other people and open new doors.

I always tell people that a mentoring session is not like going to a movie, where you sit down, watch, and walk away. The value of a mentoring session lies in the takeaways one gets from them. I tell my mentees to always carry a notebook to write down key discussion items and any action items to follow up on later.

If your mentor says something insightful, then write it down clearly. Even your mentor may not remember exactly what they said in a particular context. It is the stimulation from your conversation that may trigger new insights and thoughts from your mentors. You will be doing a great service to your mentor by capturing their insights in writing. If your mentor refers to a particular book or suggests a person that you should meet, you'll want to jot those notes down, too.

#3 – Good mentees show gratitude for their mentors

"We must find time to stop and thank the people who make a difference in our lives."

– John F Kennedy

As I mentioned earlier, time, once spent, can never be earned back. The time you've spent reading this book is gone forever. My intention and sincere hope, however, is that by mastering the art of mentoring, you'll build your career so efficiently that you save more time in the long run.

A few years ago, I taught a class on Time Management for middle school and high school students through Stanford University's Splash program, where I introduced the idea of 'investing time' versus 'wasting time.' I asked my students to list all their activities from the previous week and evaluate whether a particular activity they did was an investment of time or a waste of time.

Good mentees do everything to make their mentors feel good and valued for their time. Beyond taking notes and sending a summary, good mentees remember to thank their mentors periodically. I have also seen some mentees send physical, hand-written thank you cards to their mentors, and have heard stories about how wonderful the mentors felt when they received those cards. I have sent thank you cards to my own mentors, and have always received a delighted phone call in response.

I have seen some mentees post a tribute to their mentors via social media, after getting the mentors' permission to do so. Imagine thousands of people liking your mentors' insights. How wonderful would that be for your mentor, to be recognized by many people? This will surely make your mentors feel good, and inspire them to become more committed to the relationship.

Good mentees are also careful about not using more of their mentors' time than necessary. If your mentor gives you 45 minutes, you should be the one to call out after 40 minutes that there are five minutes remaining. I appreciate those mentees who are respectful of my time. I also make it a point to keep track of time and promptly finish the conversation at the promised time. All of this is a demonstration of respect and gratitude for your mentors.

#4 – Good mentees proactively offer help to their mentors

Even mentors need help or advice from time to time. Good mentees proactively offer to help their mentors in specific areas that the mentees are good at. For example, if you are good in writing, perhaps you can offer to proofread proposals or papers for your mentor. If you are a good online researcher, you can offer to do market research for your mentor's line of business. Or there may be a non-profit that your mentor is on the board of, and you may want to volunteer your time at this non-profit or make a contribution. Doing one or all of these shows that you as a mentee are also thinking of the value you can add to the relationship.

Rajesh Setty has also told me stories of how he offered to pick up or drop his mentors at the airport, and how he used that private time to have a great conversation.

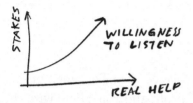

WHEN STAKES ARE HIGH,
PEOPLE LISTEN TO THOSE
WHO OFFER REAL HELP
AND ACTUALLY WALK THE TALK

SOURCE : WWW.NAPKINSIGHTS.COM /26

Good mentees make their mentoring relationships mutually beneficial, rather than a one-way street where it is always the mentor giving time, expertise, energy and connections. When you offer help and actually follow through on that promise, you earn the right to ask for help in the future.

This is an important point I need to emphasize. You don't want to gain the reputation as a free rider who only takes help and never gives. I always ask my mentees if they've helped other people in the past. I find the question to be a great qualifier, since my goal is for my mentees to eventually become great mentors, too.

To illustrate, imagine this scenario: Your mentor serves on the board of a non-profit and you, along with three or four friends, decide to volunteer at that non-profit. A week later, your mentor goes to a board meeting and is told that several volunteers, including you, came to serve at the non-profit organization's event, and all the board members offer their thanks to your mentor. Can you imagine how good your mentor would feel?

You want to remain prominent in your mentor's mind, and to continuously inspire them to do more for you. I always ask my mentors how I can help them. I have introduced my mentors to people in my network that they wanted to connect with, and have also done marketing for some of the events that my mentors organized.

#5 – Good mentees have a growth mindset and are willing to learn from their mentors

Earlier in the book, I discussed the concept of 'mindset', by Carol Dweck. Just to refresh your memory, Carol talks about two kinds of people—those with a fixed mindset and those with a growth mindset. People with a fixed mindset feel entitled to success because of their innate talents, or because they have been told repeatedly that they are smart. People with a growth mindset, on the other hand, believe in the power of effort, and recognize that results are directly dependent on the effort they put in over and above their innate skills.

Good mentees are therefore willing to work hard and pick up new skills. They do not second-guess their mentors all the time because they already have trust in them. They don't get intimidated by their mentors' success stories, and instead use them as inspiration to look inside themselves and identify ways they can improve.

#6 – Good mentees maintain confidentiality of all conversations with their mentors

This last behavior is a very important one. Mentoring is a private learning relationship between two people. I already discussed how important it is for the mentee to be open and vulnerable to make the best out of any mentoring relationship. Your mentors may also share their own stories in order to make you feel comfortable and build your confidence that challenges can be overcome with the right approach and actions.

Confidentiality is therefore very important to building and maintaining trust. After having a heart-to-heart conversation with their mentors, good mentees do not go out and discuss the conversation with 20 other people. Doing so can be detrimental to the relationship, and can be very disappointing to your mentors.

Good mentees request the same discretion from their mentors, so conversations are kept confidential on both sides.

Chapter Summary – What good mentees do

I discussed six key behaviors of good mentees. With these behaviors, good mentees eventually become great mentors over time, and it is a continuous process.

Now that you have learned all six habits of good mentees, I would like you to remember these in the form of a pledge, and refer back to this list every once in a while, in your own mentoring interactions. Place a checkmark next to the statement every time you review it, as my goal for you is to become a Stage 4 competent mentee.

Mentee Pledge:

As a good mentee –

I will – Trust my mentors and take action.

I will – Provide regular updates to my mentors.

I will – Show gratitude to my mentors.

I will – Proactively offer to help my mentors.

I will – Have a growth-mindset, and show willingness to learn from my mentors.

I will – Maintain confidentiality in all conversations with my mentors.

5   CONNECTING WITH THE RIGHT MENTORS

To sum it up in the words of Keith Ferrazzi, a globally recognized leadership guru, and author of two best sellers: *Never Eat Alone,* and *Who's Got Your Back:*

"Identify the people in your industries who always seem to be out in front, and use all the relationship skills you've acquired to connect with them."

– Keith Ferrazzi

The success of any mentoring relationship depends on finding the right mentor, assuming you are doing all the right things as a good mentee that I explained in Chapter 4. I've devised a simple, 4-step process to help you connect with the right mentors, and get them to help you achieve success.

1. Finding
2. Qualifying
3. Approaching
4. Building

#1 – Finding

You and I are living in a digital world. Popular social networks like Facebook, Twitter, Instagram, and LinkedIn allow us to connect with anyone, anytime, anywhere in the world. The challenge, then, is finding the right people to connect with—those people with the right expertise, and who are willing to invest time in you and your career.

Great mentors do not walk around with signs around their necks advertising, "I am a mentor – approach me." Some explicitly announce their interest in being a mentor on public profiles like LinkedIn or Twitter, but not many. So it's upto you to find the best ones from a very large number of people all over the world. That's where the concept of what I call 'Conscious Networking' comes into play.

Conscious networking means that you are connecting with people at conferences or via online networks with a desire to eventually find one or two potential mentors for you. You can still continue with general networking by exchanging business cards or sending invitations on LinkedIn. Beyond that, there should be a subset of people that you are consciously studying, researching, and reaching out to, who could eventually be approached for mentoring.

First, you need to identify a specific area where you need help or guidance. It may be related to your startup, your job, your academic plans, or your personal life. You should have a general idea of the challenges you are facing in these particular areas, or new opportunities that you'd like to pursue. You need to be able to describe your situation and aspirations clearly.

Second, look at your current professional and personal network, and make a list of people who you think can help you. Do not limit the possibilities by restricting yourself to the people you already know. For example, platforms like LinkedIn allow you to look at 1st, 2nd, and 3rd degree connections. You can even perform a general online search and find experts or leaders you respect and would like to have as a mentor.

From within this wide network, find at least 10 people that you can reach out to in some way. This is where you need to be realistic and bold at the same time. Be realistic in selecting those individuals you have a real chance of connecting with about the specific life or career stage you are in, and be bold in your selections of people you might not otherwise consider attempting to connect with. Take a chance; you never know what might happen.

You should also take a close look at the people you interact with on a daily basis and ask these basic questions:

- Is there someone whose work I admire?
- Have I noticed anyone who is particularly fond of helping people, giving advice, and sharing the lessons they've learned?
- Is there a colleague whose role within the company is close to a position I would like to eventually hold?
- Is there an entrepreneur that has had the success I am seeking for my own company?

Answering these questions will help to expand your initial list of people. This is the process of Conscious Networking, and it yields two valuable results:

- First, you will learn a lot more about the people around you and in your area of work;
- Second, you will learn a great deal about yourself and your specific needs.

Conferences are another great resource. When experts in your field speak on particular topics, make sure you attend and listen intently. Take notes, and highlight one or two statements that touched you. Perhaps you can tweet them later on and tag them (be absolutely sure to quote them correctly). You should also introduce yourself and have conversations with people you have never met before. Let me explain more.

A common mistake people make at conferences is to hang around only with the people they know. This is a significant misuse of the value a conference has to offer, because you can meet with your friends and colleagues anytime. Let serendipity do its work; introduce yourself to strangers, ask about their area of work, share what you do and any accomplishments you are proud of. Later, when you get home, go through the stack of cards you collected at the conference and determine if any of the people you met should be on your list of people for Conscious Networking as potential mentors.

#2 – Qualifying

Once you have a good list of individuals to work with, you need to start researching their profiles and activities. If they are active on Twitter, follow them and re-tweet anything you agree with or find as insightful. If they blog on LinkedIn, or on their own websites, add a comment or two, and show appreciation for their work and insights. If they are on the board of a local charity or a non-profit, try to get involved in case that organization's area of work is interesting to you too. You want to be noticeable to these influential people, so that when you eventually approach them to introduce yourself, they'll already know who you are. We'll touch more on this topic later in the chapter.

There are plenty of people out there who have stellar profiles on social networks, but that doesn't mean they're the person you are looking for. You need to learn how to qualify them carefully. A technique that has worked for me in the past is to study how detailed a person's LinkedIn profile is. If they highlight every tiny detail and go on and on about every small accomplishment, that should raise a flag. You're looking for the ones who talk about how they have influenced others, as well as evidence of how others have benefited from working with them.

It's easy to write about all the great things one has done and such profiles are good for attracting recruiters looking to fill open job positions. But what you're looking for is evidence that these people have helped a lot of other people, and that other people are saying great things about them. Being good at their job may not always translate directly into them being a good mentor.

By studying a potential mentor's blog or talks at conferences, you can learn a lot about their expertise and willingness to share. Their involvement with charities and other noble causes also indicates their desire to help fellow human beings. Here are some questions I ask myself before approaching someone for an initial conversation:

- Does this person have the domain expertise I am looking for? Yes/No

- Has this person achieved a level of success I hope to achieve? Yes/No

- Do I have a general idea of how to reach them? Yes/No

- Is there evidence of this person helping other people? Yes/No

- Are there one or two areas where I can directly help this person? Yes/No

- Are other people saying great things about this person? Yes/No

- Is this person currently active in the industry? Yes/No

The answers to these questions will help you come up with a shortlist of potential mentors from the longer list you created.

#3 – **Approaching**

When approaching a potential mentor for the first time, it's important to be careful and strategic, since you don't want to hurt your chances of them accepting your request. Never go up to someone and say, "I am looking to raise money for my startup", or "I need help getting a promotion", or "I am looking for a new job and need help." My best advice for getting a potential mentor to accept your request is to:

"First win their hearts, before you win their time."

Any prospective mentor should first like you and want to work with you before accepting your request to become your mentor. People have a tendency to like those who like them. I'm not talking about the "like" button on social networks, I'm talking about real connection. You are expecting someone to invest their time in you and take an active interest in your career or company. This can only happen organically, after they have enjoyed conversations with you, and you have demonstrated that you will take their advice seriously.

Get to know them, and allow them to get to know you, your values, your passion, your beliefs, your aspirations and so on—that's how you win their hearts and show that you are serious. I mentioned earlier that mentoring is a mutually rewarding and engaging conversation around a specific context. To have a good conversation, both parties should like each other, shouldn't they?

If you have followed everything outlined in the Finding and Qualifying stages of the process, it is likely that the prospective mentor will already recognize you when you approach them. They should be able to remember a comment you have added to their blog or tweet, or seen you at a charity event, or met you at a conference.

A simple rule of thumb I follow: **Always ask for 10 minutes of their time.**

Ten minutes is actually plenty of time for an initial conversation, especially if they already know something about you, and have taken an interest in you and your work.

Most good mentors enjoy being a mentor, but are always afraid that it will take too much of their time. As a result, many of them play it safe by saying they are too busy to take on a new mentee. But if they like you, and recognize that you are being respectful of their time, then they are more likely to make time for you. Do everything you can to avoid the 'I am too busy' response, especially if the individual is someone you admire for their expertise, accomplishments, and their desire to help others.

During the 10-minute conversation, you want to give the prospective mentor a general overview of what you are looking for. Directly relate your discussion to the mentor's own background and experience. For example:

"I am looking for a new career in marketing in the biotech industry, and your experience in that particular industry for 20+ years would be immensely valuable to me. You have also been a senior executive in six different companies, and the lessons you have learned along the way would help me greatly. I see that you are also a big donor at Sankara Eye Foundation, where I am also an active volunteer and regularly donate, as I believe in their cause."

In this example conversation, you have demonstrated the following:

- You have done the homework about the mentor's experience in the biotech industry

- You have studied the mentor's career path

- You have looked at the mentor's social interests and made a connection there as well

Ultimately, it is about making that 'connection' with the mentor. If you make a good, well-thought-out **connection**, it will lead to a great **conversation**.

You asked for help by first acknowledging the wisdom and heart of the mentor, and making them feel ready to help you. Having been a mentor for so many people, I can tell you what questions are going on in the mentor's mind at this point:

- Is this person worth spending my time? (**Value match**)

- Is this a good and passionate person who will benefit from my time? (**Values match**)

- How much time do I need to allocate for this person? (**Capacity match**)

- Can I actually provide the help this person needs (**Domain match**)

- Is this person at the right stage and frame of mind for me to help? (**Readiness match**)

The mentor is looking for matches along these five attributes before saying yes or no to spending more time with you. After the initial ten minutes, if they agree to meet with you again over the next couple weeks for 20-30 minutes, that is a good sign. This is how mentoring relationships evolve.

Use this same approach even when researching and approaching mentors via an online platform or email. Nothing changes except the logistics of how you take each step to win the mentor's heart and, eventually their time.

#4 – Building

Once you have succeeded in winning the heart and time of your mentor, the last and most important step is to build the relationship. I do not want you to look at mentoring as a transactional, one-time interaction with another person. It is a relationship that both you and your mentor are investing time and energy into, which will eventually generate meaningful outcomes for both of you.

A true mentoring relationship is when:

- The mentor cares, shares, helps, feels happy, and gets acknowledged for helping.

- The mentee trusts, acts, achieves measurable success, and learns a new skill.

You build that mentoring relationship by setting aside time on a weekly basis to invest in that particular relationship. In the same way we feed a fledgling plant with water and nutrients, relationships also need to be fed with the right attention at the right time, and on a continuous basis.

Remember the six best practices of good mentees? Follow them diligently, and you will have no problem building great relationships with your mentors. For example, sending a quick update email or message will ensure that you stay prominent in their mind, increasing your chances of a new introduction or opportunity. You do not want to be forgotten, and you definitely don't want to disappear after receiving their initial help.

Keep in touch and send updates. If you know that the mentor has an upcoming speaking engagement, or if it's almost their birthday, send them your good wishes. Even if there is nothing specific you need, just send a quick hello message and ask about the mentor's well-being and family.

Taking a prominent place in the mind of your mentors has numerous advantages. To illustrate, let me explain how the world has changed over the past few decades when it comes to networking and connecting with people.

4 dimensions of building relationships

Who knows you

What you know

Who you know

What strengths of yours do they know

During the post WWII era, you got recognized and earned employment based on **What You Know**. Your education, technical skills, and experience played a key role in getting a job.

In the 1990's and 2000's, the priority shifted to **Who You Know**. In spite of having the best education, skills, and expertise, you still needed someone to refer you for a particular job opening. Thanks to the sudden explosion of online recruiting platforms, any given job opening received thousands of applications from all over the world. Knowing someone who worked within the firm you were seeking to join made a big difference in your chances of getting a job.

In today's world, what matters a great deal is **Who Knows You**. Who are those business leaders and highly successful entrepreneurs that know you, your skills, your aspirations, and your values? It is not enough to have hundreds or even thousands of people on your Facebook, LinkedIn, or Twitter accounts. These are people you know and have connected with. But think about these questions:

- How many of those know you really well?

- How many will bring up your name or your needs in their conversations?

- How many are thinking about how best to help you?

- How many have a vested interest in your success?

Having 10-15 notable people who fall into one or all of these four categories will be invaluable for you. It will not happen all by itself; it takes diligence and strategic planning over time to build a list of people like that.

I want to emphasize one particular aspect of your mentors mentioning you in their conversations with others in their network. What your mentor says about you is critical. Your mentor should not only be aware of your immediate needs, but also your strengths and your passion.

Early on in my entrepreneurial journey, I was often perceived as a nice person. There was nothing wrong with that evaluation in itself, of course, but it was a soft perception that lacked any depth. Let me give some real examples:

- There was no conversation about my big vision to connect 100 million mentors and mentees by 2020.

- There was no discussion of the successes I had with very little resources.

- They didn't know I worked on the Boeing 787 Dreamliner.

- They didn't remember that I was featured in Harvard Business Review and Forbes.

- They didn't know I was invited by Hillary Clinton to speak in the U.S. State Department.

I realized my mistake. I was failing to make my story 'transportable,' as my mentor Rajesh would say. Rajesh would always encourage me to tell a story that others could easily remember and share.

Instead of sharing my story in a clear and concise way, I would often share too much all at once, so my mentors wouldn't know which areas to stress upon. It is your job as a mentee to share your story in a way that allows people to tell it to others. That is when the needle is likely to move in ways you cannot comprehend or imagine.

By staying engaged, being in regular communication, providing updates, helping your mentors or their causes when appropriate, and giving them transportable stories, you can build a productive, long-lasting relationship with your mentors.

COMMUNICATION HAS 2 PARTS
(a) TRANSMISSION
(b) RECEPTION
GOOD COMMUNICATORS TAKE
RESPONSIBILITY FOR BOTH PARTS

TRANSMISSION   RECEPTION

SOURCE : WWW. NAPKINSIGHT · COM /56

In addition to the four steps of finding, qualifying, approaching, and building relationships with great mentors, there are two additional ideas on the topic of connecting with the right mentors. I consider these two ideas to be the most important, and my personal favorites. Let me call them Idea A and Idea B.

Idea A – Personal Board of Mentors

It is a fact of life that I can't possibly know everything there is to know. There are many books I haven't read, places I haven't visited, experiences I haven't had, people I haven't met, and subjects I haven't studied.

My education and experience is limited, and in the complex world you and I live in, it is impossible to navigate life all by ourselves. Finding balance in all areas of life —personal, financial, professional, family, health, spiritual, and so on—leads to a happy and successful life. Having someone to depend on for advice and perspective can help avoid mistakes in each of these key areas.

If you have one go-to person that you trust as a mentor for each of these areas, then all of them together is what I call your 'Personal Board of Mentors.'

THE MOST EXPENSIVE HABIT IS TO LEARN ONLY FROM DIRECT EXPERIENCE

SOURCE : WWW.NAPKINSIGHT.COM /255

These are the people you have personally chosen, and those who have a vested interest in your success. You need to at least know who to call and discuss your challenges with. It is rare that one or two individuals alone possess enough wisdom to guide you in all of the areas of life.

To demonstrate, take a look at any private or public company. They each have a management team to run day-to-day operations, and a Board of Directors (BOD) to advise the management team on operational and strategic matters. A company usually has one board member for go-to-market strategy, one representing the investors, one to advise on technology, one to guide on people and talent issues, and one focusing on financial matters, and so on. The BOD has a vested interest in the company's success, and the members are all experienced individuals carefully selected by the management team.

I am sure you've heard the saying that you are the CEO (Chief Executive Officer) of your own life. In that case, shouldn't you have your own personal Board of Mentors to help you navigate through the challenges and new opportunities that come your way? Who are you going to call if you have a professional career issue? Calling people out of the blue and asking for help rarely works. Even if someone offered you on-the-fly help in your career, it may not be the best piece of advice, since it was given to you in a rush.

Friends might offer advice if you ask them, but even though they have good intentions, their advice may not always be the best for you. Their advice will depend on their own personal experiences, and they may not have seen enough in their own career to be able to guide you properly. It is therefore far better to identify people you can rely on as mentors, that you can go to for help. These should be people you have an ongoing relationship with, who can recognize who's on the other end when the phone rings.

Idea B – Being found by great mentors

Just like a teacher is delighted when they find a good student, good mentors also love to work with good people who can grow into becoming good mentees. We've already gone over the six habits of good mentees, but there is more you can do once a mentoring relationship has begun in order to ensure its success, as well as the success of future mentoring relationships you may enter into.

First, be an enthusiastic and positive person to begin with. Make yourself known in the community or the organization you belong to by sharing your ideas through a blog, via micro-blogging sites like Twitter, or by volunteering your time. Having a robust LinkedIn profile is also important these days so people can find you.

Second, be a mentor to other people. How can you have the heart to ask for help when you yourself have not helped anyone? By being a good mentor yourself, you can be appreciated by good mentors who may eventually want to work with you.

To be loved, you must love others first.

To get, you must give first.

To be thanked, you must thank first.

To be a good parent, you must be a good child first.

To be a good teacher, you must be a good student first.

To be mentored, you must mentor first.

My own stories as a mentor inspire my mentors. My experience with Srikanth Bolla, a visually challenged student who I mentored to get into MIT, and to eventually become a successful social entrepreneur, is a story that attracts my mentors. I have personally mentored over 100 students and early-career professionals, and those stories inspire excitement in my mentors to want to work with me.

I challenge and urge you to be a mentor to someone else. In turn, you earn the right to seek mentoring from someone else. The secret to finding and getting connected with great mentors is to be a great mentor yourself for other people who can benefit from your wisdom. We each have something to share with others. Great mentors are drawn to other great people, and you should be so good at what you do, what you say, and what you stand for, that good mentors naturally want to work with you and help you get ahead.

6 BENEFITS OF MENTORING

Now that we've defined mentoring and discussed the myths surrounding it, described several key behaviors of good mentors and mentees, and discussed at length the process and strategy of finding and connecting with good mentors, let me bring it all together by explaining the true benefits of mentoring.

You are reading this book and have come this far because you recognize the value of mentoring. What I want to do now is explain in my own words and from my own experience what that value is. I hope it will help you articulate the value of mentoring to other people, when the time comes.

Mentoring is one form of Accelerated Learning

Let me expand by offering a few examples:

Let's say you wanted to learn something quickly. Would you rather learn on your own by picking up a big book and spending three to four months reading it, or sign up for a class (online or offline) with a professor who has studied the subject for years? The professor will not only teach you the concepts, but also provide context and test your knowledge with quizzes and evaluations, a much quicker method than studying all on your own.

Another example: If you want to drive to a particular destination in a new unknown territory, would you prefer being heroic and driving around on your own, or using a Global Positioning System (GPS) device to guide you? A GPS device incorporates intelligence from multiple sources: aerial maps, traffic conditions, the presence of other cars in the area, any construction activity or accidents, and so on. Leveraging that aggregated intelligence is a smart way to avoid getting into a traffic jam or getting lost, and will get you to your destination much quicker than trying to find your way on your own.

In a similar manner, mentoring is a form of accelerated learning. Whether you are an entrepreneur working on your startup, a student preparing for an interview, a successful professional seeking a job promotion, or someone looking to change your career, it is wise to speak with someone who has had practical, hands-on experience, and who also cares about your success.

People say that hindsight is 20/20, but you cannot afford to build your career strictly through your own hindsight. Working with someone as a mentor is smart, because you are learning from another individual's hindsight. Your mentor's hindsight can be your 20/20 looking into the future. It will help you avoid common mistakes, and greatly increase the odds and pace of your success.

Mentoring conversations typically happen in a domain where you have some previous education, exposure, and experience. It rarely happens that your mentor is teaching you a new concept or subject that you have never heard of. For such topics, you are better off taking a class with a professor or at any of the numerous online learning sites like Coursera, Udacity, Udemy. The goal is to avoid wasting your mentor's time.

Choose 1.
- O Learning in the present
- O Mediocrity in the future

John Doe.

Making learning optional in the present is to sign a contract for mediocrity in the future

SOURCE: WWW.NAPKINSIGHTS.COM / 13

But if the topic you are discussing with your mentor is an area in which you have prior knowledge and some experience, then mentoring helps you to quickly take your game to the next level.

What you really need is for someone to validate your approach, suggest a new tactic or strategy, open doors, question your thinking, or help you get better at what you are already doing. In all these cases, learning will be much faster with the help of a mentor, compared to you reading whole books or taking courses on the subject. Especially if you are an entrepreneur trying to refine your storytelling, improve your pitch, or change your go-to-market strategy, you do not have the option of taking time away from your company and enrolling in a class.

In general, it is better to be a good player in an ecosystem than to be the best in a silo

SOURCE : WWW.NAPKINSIGHT.COM/256

If you are already in the game, then a mentor can give you additional tips and strategies, so you can quickly take your game to the next level, which is exactly why mentoring is an invaluable tool to accelerate your learning and skill development.

Mentoring Conversations Open New Doors and Expand Possibilities

I talked about this as one of the key traits of good mentors, but want to emphasize it as a major benefit of mentoring.

Being in a mentoring relationship is an opportunity to have intelligent, insightful, and inspiring conversations. This is how it has been for me, working with my mentors and mentees alike. If you do all the right things in picking your mentors and mentees, using all the best practices I discussed in the last three chapters, then I guarantee you will have fun and see growth from working with your mentors and mentees.

I found from my own experience that true wisdom is unleashed only during insightful conversations with the right people and in the right context. It is impossible for me to write down everything I know. Even with all the knowledge and wisdom inside my brain, I may not even be aware that I know something until another person asks me about it and challenges me to ponder on it. That is the power of mentoring.

Let me illustrate with an example that is not directly related to mentoring.

I know the directions to go from San Jose downtown to San Francisco airport. Even though that information is hidden in my brain, it is unlikely that I will tell the whole world about it. It is only when someone asks me for directions that I am prompted to recollect and share that information.

In a mentoring conversation too, because of the topic and context, your brain has the power to go deep and recollect a multitude of information from all the books you have read, people you have met, videos you have watched, or stories you have heard. Unless you are writing a book, all that wisdom gets tapped into and shared only when you are talking in context with a mentor and mentee. The spontaneity of the conversation has the potential for new wisdom to be discovered, new connections to be made, and new doors to be opened.

This book is a direct evidence. My mentors and mentees always acknowledged something that I said during our conversations and encouraged me to write this book. If not for the value I gained from my own mentoring conversations, the ideas in this book would never have seen the light of day or made it into your hands. There is tremendous value in engaging in intelligent and insightful conversations with others.

Possibilities on the other side

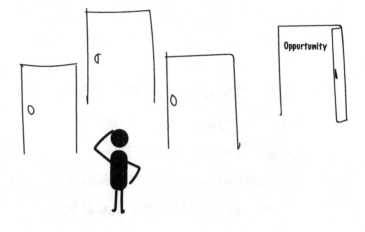

Amazing things have happened to me in my own entrepreneurial journey through conversations with my mentors. I got to be on a panel at the World Demographic Forum in Switzerland. I was invited by Hillary Clinton when she was the U.S. Secretary of State to deliver a plenary talk on mentoring. I was interviewed for articles in Forbes and the Harvard Business Review. All of these unforgettable events happened because of intellectual conversations, and those conversations leading to new doors being opened by mentors and friends.

THE TRAGEDY IS NOT THE LESSON YOU MISSED LEARNING, BUT THE LEARNING OPPORTUNITIES YOU MISSED NOTICING.

SOURCE : WWW.NAPKINSIGHTS.COM/30

Mentoring Builds Your Leadership Skills, Legacy, and Brand

The #1 myth about mentoring is that it only benefits the mentee, because it's the mentor who is pouring all of their knowledge, discipline, and expertise into the mentee. This is simply not true, and I debunked this myth already in the first chapter. The bigger benefactor in a mentoring relationship is actually the mentor. People who help others grow will in turn grow in their own careers. Being a good mentor is a direct reflection of your leadership in your domain or organization.

Being a mentor is also a great way to build your legacy. If you do not share your knowledge with anyone, how will others know what you know?

Sharing your knowledge as a mentor builds credibility. It also serves as validation for your knowledge and expertise. It helps you curate your own mind to distinguish between what you know and what you do not know, which helps you then to leverage your strengths and work on any weaknesses.

If you are a senior executive in a company who did not grow up with technology like millennials today, you can learn a lot by mentoring a young person in your organization. Millennials grew up with technology such as smartphones, 3D printing, social media, self-driving cars, drones, robots, gaming, and much more. You as the mentor have the direct benefit of learning about these new and latest technologies when you work with a mentee from a different generation.

In a give-take relationship, it is the giver who often gets recognized and remembered. In the case of mentoring, too, it is the mentor people remember for a long time.

As a mentor, you also benefit from growing your personal brand. Your reputation as a leader in your area of expertise, and as one who fosters the growth of others through mentorship, will spread throughout your field. More people will see you as a role model and want to work with you.

I have garnered the respect of countless people thanks to all the mentees I have had the privilege of working with. The stories I am able to share inspire people, and my relationships have only gotten stronger because of what I was able to do for other people.

Mentoring Creates Great Stories You Can Tell

Storytelling is by far the most important skill today. No one has time to spend hours researching your resume or startup or professional experience to fully understand who you really are. But if you can communicate your strengths, beliefs, work, and vision via stories, people will be drawn to you and remember you.

I have had the privilege of mentoring many remarkable individuals. Srikanth Bolla, the 16-year-old visually-challenged student from Hyderabad, India is someone I had the pleasure of mentoring as a teenager through to launching his first company and this is a story I am delighted to tell over and over again. And he's not the only one. I have many more such stories of people I was able to help, who have transformed me personally as a leader, entrepreneur, and human being.

I realized the power I had to transform the lives of other people just by spending a few minutes with them each week and tapping into the knowledge I had sitting in my head that wouldn't otherwise be leveraged.

The true power of mentoring is not a feeling I can articulate to you. It is something you need to experience first-hand. For example, I can never fully describe the taste of ice cream, can I? The sweetness of gratification and self-worth through mentorship is similar, and I hope you create many of your own stories to tell. Whether you are raising money for your company or interviewing for a job, your mentoring stories can be integral to demonstrating the real 'you.'

Your resume can summarize all your educational qualifications, professional accomplishments, certifications, and so on, but it can never do enough to describe the goodness in your heart, which can only be shared through a story about you helping others get ahead in their lives.

Take some time now and list all the people you have personally helped. Write down how you helped them. Most importantly, write down if they will acknowledge your help if I sent them an email or called them.

Name	How you helped?	Will they acknowledge your help?

Now think of the people who have helped you.

Name	How they helped?	Have you acknowledged their help?

Do any new stories come to mind through this exercise? Stories about your travels to exotic places are fine for social excitement, but what about the stories of you helping other people in their careers, life situations, startups, academics? Imagine this –

- Someone got a career promotion because of you

- Someone got a better grade because of you

- Someone closed a new deal because of you

- Someone raised funding because of you

- Someone is happier because of you

Tell the stories that grow from your work through helping others as a mentor, and continue to add to those stories. These are the stories that will define who you are, and continue to elevate your leadership, legacy, brand, and self-worth.

BIBLIOGRAPHY

Rajagopalachari, Chakravarti. *Mahabharata*. Chaupatty,
    Bombay: Bharatiya Vidya Bhavan, 1958.

Murrell, Audrey J., Forte-Trammell, Sheila., and Bing, Diana.
    *Intelligent Mentoring: How IBM Creates Value through People,
    Knowledge, and Relationships* (IBM Press) Paperback – 2008.

Dweck, Carol S. *Mindset: The New Psychology of Success.*
    New York: Random House, 2006.

Gladwell, Malcolm. *Outliers: The Story of Success.*
    New York: Little, Brown, 2008.

Lance, H.K. Secretan. *The Spark, the Flame, and the Torch: Inspire Self.
    Inspire Others. Inspire the World.* 2010.

Gardner, Chris, Quincy Troupe, and Mim Eichler. Rivas.
    The Pursuit of Happyness. New York: Amistad, 2006.

Covey, Stephen M. R., and Rebecca R. Merrill. *The Speed of Trust:
    The One Thing That Changes Everything.* New York: Free, 2006.

Ferrazzi, Keith, and Tahl Raz. *Never Eat Alone: And Other Secrets to
Success, One Relationship at a Time.*
    New York: Crown Business, 2014.

Ferrazzi, Keith. *Who's Got Your Back: The Breakthrough Program to
Build Deep, Trusting Relationships That Create Success--* and *Won't Let
You Fail.*
    New York: Broadway, 2009.

Sammy Lee. *The Autopilot Leadership Model.*
    McGraw Hill Education. 2016.

INDEX